1200 CALORIE DIET FOR

BEGGINER

The Ultimate daily meal plan to lose 50 pounds in 30 days with high protein recipes and low carb recipes.

MAGERET LAWRENCE PHD

TABLE OF CONTENT

INTRODUCTION 7

CHAPTER ONE 10

Explanation of the 1200 calorie diet 10

Who is this diet suitable for? 12

Benefits of a 1200 calorie diet 14

CHAPTER TWO 17

Understanding Nutrition 17

Macros and micros nutrition 19

Importance of a balanced diet 22

CHAPTER THREE 29

Meal Plan 29

Daily meal structure 33

Recipes for each meal 34

Nutritional information for each meal 38

CHAPTER FOUR 41

Breakfast 41

CHAPTER FIVE 45

Recipe for each breakfast................................. 45

Sliced banana and whole-grain cereal with low-fat milk.
.... 45

Veggie and Cheese Omelet............................. 46

Berry and Yogurt Smoothie............................. 47

Sliced banana and whole-grain toast with peanut butter.
.... 49

Nutritional information for each breakfast 51

CHAPTER SIX 57

Lunch 57

lunch.. 58

Grilled Chicken Salad:.................................... 58

Turkey and Avocado Wrap:............................... 60

Veggie wrap:.. 61

Recipes for each lunch.................................... 64

Grilled chicken salad recipe............................. 64

Turkey and Avocado Wrap recipe 66

Veggie wrap recipe. 67

Nutritional information for each lunch 70

CHAPTER SEVEN 73

Dinner 73

dinner options... 74

Recipes for each dinner... 75

Nutritional information for each dinner........................ 86

CHAPTER EIGHT 94

Snacks 94

Recipes for each snack.. 95

Fresh fruit... 95

Raw veggies 97

Yogurt: 98

Nut: 99

Rice crackers:.. 100

Nutritional information for each snack........................ 102

Fresh fruit salad.. 102

Yogurt 103

Nut... 105

Rice cracker 106

CHAPTER NINE...107

Staying on Track.. 107

Strategies for success 109

Handling cravings 111

Incorporating physical activity into your routine........ 112

CONCLUSION...114

Summary of benefits 114

Encouragement for success...................................... 116

Final thoughts and tips. 118

INTRODUCTION

Jamie was a man in his late 30s who had always struggled with his weight. He tried so hard to lose the extra weight, but just couldn't seem to do it. He tried various diets and exercise plans, but nothing seemed to work.

One day, a friend recommended the 1200 calorie diet to Jamie. At first, he was skeptical. He had heard of low-calorie diets before, and they always seemed too restrictive and boring. But his friend promised him that this was different, and that he would see results if he stuck with it.

So, Jamie decided to give it a try. He purchased a 1200 calorie meal plan book and got to work. The first thing he noticed was how easy the meal plan was to follow. The recipes were simple, yet delicious, and he was never hungry. He was amazed at how much food he could eat while still staying within his daily calorie limit.

Jamie also incorporated physical activity into his routine. He started by taking daily walks and gradually built up to more intense workouts. This not only helped him burn more calories, but also gave him more energy and improved his overall sense of well-being.

As the weeks passed, Jamie noticed a gradual reduction in weight. He was amazed at how quickly he was seeing results. He was also feeling better than ever before, with improved energy levels and a clearer mind.

After several months of following the 1200 calorie diet, Jamie had reached his goal weight. He was thrilled with his progress and couldn't believe how easy it had been. He had finally found the diet that worked for him, and he was feeling healthier, happier, and more confident than ever before.

From that day on, Jamie continued to follow the 1200 calorie diet and maintain his weight loss. He was grateful for the positive impact it had on his life and was happy to recommend it to others.

Jamie soon realized that the 1200 calorie diet was not just a quick fix, but a lifestyle change. He learned to make healthier food choices and incorporate physical activity into his routine. He found that he no longer craved unhealthy foods and that he felt better when he ate nutritious, whole foods.

He also discovered the importance of portion control and how it helped him maintain his weight loss. By following the meal plan, he was able to control his portions and avoid overeating, which was key to his success.

As time went on, Jamie became an advocate for the 1200 calorie diet and shared his story with others. He was amazed at how many people he inspired to make positive changes in their own lives. He felt proud to be a role model for healthy living and was happy to share his success with others.

Jamie's weight loss journey was not only about losing pounds, but also about gaining confidence, improving his health, and finding happiness. He was grateful for the positive impact that the 1200 calorie diet had on his life and was eager to help others achieve the same success.

From that day on, Jamie continued to live a healthy and active lifestyle. He was proud of himself for sticking to the 1200 calorie diet and was happy to see the positive impact it had on his life. He was finally at peace with his body and felt confident in his own skin.

CHAPTER ONE

Explanation of the 1200 calorie diet

The 1200 calorie diet is a popular weight loss plan that involves reducing your daily caloric intake to 1200 calories. The goal of this diet is to create a calorie deficit, which means consuming fewer calories than your body burns, leading to weight loss.

The 1200 calorie diet typically consists of 3 meals and 2 snacks per day, with each meal containing approximately 400 calories. The meal plan usually includes a variety of healthy foods, including lean protein, whole grains, fruits, and vegetables, as well as low-fat dairy products. The diet also restricts the intake of high-calorie, high-fat, and sugary foods.

It's important to note that individual calorie needs may vary based on factors such as age, gender, weight, and physical activity level. Consulting a doctor or a registered dietitian is recommended before starting any weight loss plan, especially if you have any health conditions or concerns.

The 1200 calorie diet can be effective for weight loss in the short term, but it may not be sustainable for the long-term and may result in boredom and lack of essential nutrients. It's crucial to maintain a balanced and varied diet while also engaging in regular physical activity to achieve and maintain a healthy weight.

Additionally, it's important to be mindful of portion sizes and to avoid skipping meals, as this can slow down your metabolism and result in overeating later.

It's also recommended to drink plenty of water and limit the consumption of alcohol and other calorie-dense beverages. In conclusion, the 1200 calorie diet can be a useful tool for weight loss, but it should be followed under the supervision of a healthcare professional and in combination with a nutritious, balanced diet and regular exercise.

It's important to make gradual and sustainable changes to your diet and lifestyle to achieve and maintain a healthy weight over time.

Who is this diet suitable for?

The 1200 calorie diet is suitable for adult men who are overweight or obese and want to lose weight. It can also be suitable for men who have a sedentary lifestyle and need to reduce their calorie intake to maintain a healthy weight. However, it's important to note that individual calorie needs may vary based on factors such as age, weight, height, muscle mass, and physical activity level.

It's recommended to consult a doctor or a registered dietitian before starting any weight loss plan, especially if you have any health conditions or concerns. Men with certain health conditions, such as diabetes or kidney disease, may need to modify the diet to meet their specific needs.

In general, the 1200 calorie diet is not recommended for athletes or highly active men, as they may require more calories to fuel their physical activity and support muscle growth and repair. Also, men who are underweight or have a history of disordered eating should avoid this diet and seek guidance from a healthcare professional.

It's important to understand that the 1200 calorie diet is a low-calorie diet and may not provide enough nutrients and energy for men with a high level of physical activity or those who are highly active in their daily lives. For these men, a higher calorie intake may be necessary to meet their energy needs and support optimal health and well-being.

Additionally, following a restrictive diet for a prolonged period can result in decreased metabolism and nutrient deficiencies, which can negatively impact overall health. It's essential to adopt a well-balanced diet that includes a variety of nutrient-dense foods to ensure that you're getting all the essential vitamins, minerals, and nutrients your body needs.

In summary, the 1200 calorie diet may be suitable for some adult men who are overweight or obese and want to lose weight, but it's important to seek guidance from a healthcare professional and to make sure that the diet is balanced and meets all of your nutrient needs. Making gradual and sustainable changes to your diet and lifestyle, such as increasing physical activity and adopting healthy eating habits, can help you achieve and maintain a healthy weight over time.

Benefits of a 1200 calorie diet

The main benefit of a 1200 calorie diet for men is weight loss. By reducing caloric intake, this diet creates a calorie deficit, which can lead to weight loss over time. Additionally, a 1200 calorie diet may also help improve some health markers, such as:

Blood pressure: By reducing the intake of high-sodium and high-fat foods, a 1200 calorie diet may help lower blood pressure levels.

Blood sugar control: By emphasizing low-glycemic index foods and reducing sugar intake, a 1200 calorie diet may improve blood sugar control for men with diabetes or prediabetes.

Cholesterol levels: By limiting the intake of saturated and trans fats, a 1200 calorie diet may improve cholesterol levels and reduce the risk of heart disease.

Better digestion: By including fiber-rich foods such as whole grains, fruits, and vegetables, a 1200 calorie diet may improve digestion and regularity.

It's important to note that individual results may vary and that the effectiveness of a 1200 calorie diet for weight loss and health improvement will depend on factors such as the individual's starting weight, physical activity level, and overall diet and lifestyle habits.

In conclusion, a 1200 calorie diet can be beneficial for weight loss and improved health markers for some adult men who are overweight or obese. However, it's important to seek guidance from a healthcare professional to make sure that the diet is balanced and meets all of your nutrient needs, and to adopt healthy habits that can be sustained over the long-term.

It's also worth mentioning that a 1200 calorie diet can serve as a starting point for making changes to one's diet and lifestyle, with the goal of adopting healthier habits that can be sustained over the long-term. Making gradual and sustainable changes, such as reducing portion sizes, increasing physical activity, and choosing nutrient-dense foods, can help improve overall health and prevent weight gain in the future.

Additionally, following a 1200 calorie diet can help individuals become more mindful of their food choices and develop better eating habits, such as avoiding processed foods, sugary drinks, and excessive portions. These habits can lead to improved health, not only in terms of weight loss but also in terms of overall wellness.

It's also important to keep in mind that weight loss is not the only measure of success when it comes to a healthy lifestyle. Improved energy levels, better sleep, increased physical fitness, and improved mental health can also be positive outcomes of adopting a healthy diet and lifestyle.

In conclusion, a 1200 calorie diet can provide weight loss and other health benefits for some men, but it's important to seek guidance from a healthcare professional, make sustainable changes, and adopt healthy habits that can be sustained over the long-term. Weight loss should not be the only focus, but rather a part of a comprehensive approach to overall health and wellness.

CHAPTER TWO

Understanding Nutrition

The study of nutrition focuses on how food influences the body. It includes understanding how nutrients are processed and utilized by the body, how different foods contribute to overall health and well-being, and how diet and lifestyle choices can prevent or manage various health conditions. Key nutrients include carbohydrates, proteins, fats, vitamins, and minerals, and it's important to consume a balanced diet that provides the necessary amount of these nutrients to meet the body's needs.

Maintaining overall health and wellbeing requires a healthy diet. It plays a vital role in maintaining a healthy weight, supporting physical activity and growth, and helping to prevent chronic diseases such as heart disease, diabetes, and certain types of clike heart disease, diabetes, and specific forms of cancer..

A balanced diet should consist of a variety of foods from all food groups, including fruits and vegetables, whole grains, lean proteins, and low-fat dairy. It is important to consume the recommended daily allowances of key nutrients such as vitamins, minerals, and fiber.

In addition to providing essential nutrients, a healthy diet can also have a positive impact on mental health. Studies have shown that a diet rich in fruits, vegetables, whole grains, and lean protein can help reduce symptoms of depression and anxiety and improve overall mood.

However, it is also important to be mindful of portion sizes and calorie intake, as consuming too many calories can lead to weight gain and other health problems. Additionally, consuming high amounts of unhealthy foods such as added sugars and saturated fats can increase the risk of chronic diseases.

It is recommended to consult a registered dietitian or a healthcare provider to develop a personalized nutrition plan based on individual needs and goals. This can help ensure that you are consuming a balanced and nutritious diet that meets your body's needs and supports good health.

Macros and micros nutrition

Macronutrients and micronutrients are two important categories of nutrients that the body needs in order to function properly.

Macronutrients include carbohydrates, proteins, and fats and are needed in large amounts to provide energy and support the growth and maintenance of the body's tissues. Carbohydrates are the body's primary source of energy and are found in foods such as bread, pasta, rice, and fruits. Proteins, which are present in foods like meat, poultry, fish, eggs, and dairy products, are crucial for the development and repair of tissues. Fats are important for storing energy, maintaining cell structure, and aiding in the absorption of fat-soluble vitamins.

Micronutrients, on the other hand, include vitamins and minerals and are needed in smaller amounts but are still essential for good health. Vitamins and minerals play important roles in various bodily functions, such as supporting a strong immune system, maintaining healthy bones, and aiding in the metabolism of macronutrients. Micronutrients can be found in a variety of foods, including fruits and vegetables, dairy products, and fortified foods.

Both macronutrients and micronutrients are important for good health, and a balanced diet should include a variety of foods that provide the necessary amounts of both.

It is important to consume the right balance of macronutrients and micronutrients for optimal health and well-being. An excess or deficiency of any one macronutrient can have negative health effects. For example, a diet high in saturated fats can increase the risk of heart disease, while a diet low in carbohydrates can lead to fatigue and decreased physical performance.

Micronutrient deficiencies can also have serious consequences. For example, a lack of vitamin C can lead to scurvy, while a deficiency in iron can cause anemia. A diet lacking in essential vitamins and minerals can also weaken the immune system and increase the risk of chronic diseases. It is important to consult a registered dietitian or healthcare provider for personalized recommendations on macronutrient and micronutrient intake, as needs can vary based on age, gender, and individual health conditions. Additionally, it is recommended to consume a variety of nutrient-dense foods to ensure that the body is receiving an adequate amount of both macronutrients and micronutrients.

In conclusion, macronutrients and micronutrients are both essential for good health, and a balanced diet should include a variety of foods that provide the necessary amounts of both. Proper nutrition can help maintain overall health, prevent chronic diseases, and support physical and mental well-being.

Importance of a balanced diet

For overall health and wellbeing, a balanced diet is necessary. It provides the body with the nutrients it needs to function properly and maintain optimal health. A balanced diet is one that includes a variety of foods from all food groups in the right proportions, providing the necessary amounts of macronutrients (carbohydrates, proteins, and fats) and micronutrients (vitamins and minerals).

Maintains a healthy weight: A balanced diet provides the body with the energy it needs to function properly and supports weight management. Consuming a diet high in fruits, vegetables, whole grains, and lean protein, and low in added sugars and unhealthy fats, can help maintain a healthy weight.

Supports physical health: A balanced diet provides the necessary nutrients for physical health, such as vitamins and minerals that are essential for building and repairing tissues, supporting the immune system, and maintaining healthy bones. It also provides the energy needed for physical activity.

Prevents chronic diseases: Consuming a balanced diet can help prevent chronic diseases such as heart disease, diabetes, and certain types of cancer. A diet rich in fruits, vegetables, whole grains, and lean protein and low in unhealthy fats and added sugars can reduce the risk of chronic diseases.

Supports mental health: Studies have shown that a balanced diet can have a positive impact on mental health. A diet rich in fruits, vegetables, whole grains, and lean protein has been shown to reduce symptoms of depression and anxiety and improve overall mood.

Promotes digestive health: A balanced diet provides the necessary fiber and water to support digestive health. Fiber helps regulate digestion and prevent constipation, while water helps maintain hydration and promotes regular bowel movements.

Supports cognitive function: A balanced diet provides the necessary nutrients for brain function, such as omega-3 fatty acids and B-vitamins. These nutrients support memory and concentration and can help reduce the risk of cognitive decline.

It is important to consult a registered dietitian or healthcare provider for personalized recommendations on macronutrient and micronutrient intake, as needs can vary based on age, gender, and individual health conditions. Additionally, it is recommended to consume a variety of nutrient-dense foods to ensure that the body is receiving an adequate amount of both macronutrients and micronutrients. The key to overall health and wellbeing is a balanced diet.. Consuming a variety of nutrient-dense foods in the right proportions can help maintain physical and mental health, prevent chronic diseases, and support a healthy weight.

It is important to note that a balanced diet is not a one-size-fits-all approach and that individual nutritional needs can vary based on factors such as age, gender, activity level, and health conditions. For example, older adults may require more calcium and vitamin D for healthy bones, while athletes may require a higher protein intake to support muscle recovery and growth.

To achieve a balanced diet, it is recommended to follow the guidelines set by organizations such as the United States Department of Agriculture (USDA) and the World Health Organization (WHO). These guidelines recommend consuming a variety of foods from each food group, including:

Fruits and vegetables: aim for at least 5 servings per day, as they are rich in vitamins, minerals, and fiber.

Grains: choose whole grains, such as whole wheat bread, brown rice, and oatmeal, as they are rich in fiber, vitamins, and minerals.

Proteins: choose lean proteins, such as chicken, fish, and legumes, and aim to consume at least 2 servings per day.

Dairy: aim for 3 servings per day of dairy products, such as milk, yogurt, and cheese, as they are rich in calcium and vitamin D.

Fats: choose healthy fats, such as those found in nuts, seeds, and avocados, and limit saturated and trans fats.

It is also important to limit the consumption of added sugars, salt, and unhealthy fats. Added sugars are often found in processed and sugary foods and drinks, while unhealthy fats are found in foods such as fried foods and processed snack foods. Excessive salt intake can lead to high blood pressure and increase the risk of heart disease.

In addition to following dietary guidelines, it is also important to be mindful of portion sizes and to avoid overeating. A balanced diet does not mean eating unlimited amounts of food, but rather consuming the right balance of nutrients in the right amounts to support good health.

In conclusion, a balanced diet is a crucial component of overall health and well-being. By following dietary guidelines and consuming a variety of nutrient-dense foods, individuals can support physical and mental health, prevent chronic diseases, and maintain a healthy weight. A consultation with a registered dietitian or healthcare provider can provide personalized recommendations for optimal nutrition.

Here are some additional food choices that can be included in a 1200 calorie diet:

Eggs: Boiled, scrambled, or poached eggs are a great source of protein and can be paired with whole grain toast for a balanced breakfast.

Leafy greens: Spinach, kale, and arugula are low in calories and high in fiber, vitamins, and minerals. They can be added to smoothies, salads, or sautéed as a side dish.

Nuts and seeds: Almonds, walnuts, chia seeds, and pumpkin seeds are a good source of healthy fats, fiber, and protein. They can be added to oatmeal, yogurt, or consumed as a snack.

Tuna: Canned tuna in water is a low-calorie, high-protein food that can be added to salads, sandwiches, or paired with whole grain crackers.

Berries: Strawberries, blueberries, and raspberries are low in calories and high in fiber, vitamins, and antioxidants. They can be eaten as a snack or added to yogurt or oatmeal.

Sweet potatoes: sweet potatoes are a good source of complex carbohydrates, fiber, and vitamins. They can be roasted, mashed, or baked as a side dish.

Chicken breast: Skinless, boneless chicken breast is a low-calorie, high-protein food that can be grilled, baked, or stir-fried.

Beans: Lentils, black beans, and chickpeas are a good source of protein, fiber, and complex

carbohydrates. They can be added to soups, salads, or paired with brown rice for a balanced meal.

It is important to remember that these food choices are not an exhaustive list and there are many other nutrient-dense foods that can be included in a 1200 calorie diet.

When following a calorie-restricted diet, it is also important to drink plenty of water, avoid sugary drinks, and limit alcohol consumption.

Consultation with a registered dietitian or healthcare provider can provide personalized recommendations for optimal nutrition.

CHAPTER THREE

Meal Plan

A meal plan is a comprehensive guide to healthy eating that outlines what foods to eat and in what quantities, based on an individual's specific nutritional needs and goals. Whether it's for weight loss, weight management, or to improve overall health, a well-planned meal plan can help achieve optimal nutrition and wellness.

Creating a meal plan considers the individual's calorie needs, macronutrient requirements, food preferences, and any dietary restrictions. It helps to eliminate the guesswork and stress of meal planning and provides a roadmap for making healthier food choices.

A meal plan can also help to promote healthy habits, such as eating regularly and avoiding junk food, and can lead to a more balanced and satisfying diet.

It is important to note that a meal plan should not be a rigid, restrictive plan, but rather a flexible guide that can be adjusted based on changes in appetite, lifestyle, or personal preferences. The goal of a meal plan is to provide a balanced and nutritious diet, not to limit food choices or restrict calorie intake.

A meal plan is a valuable tool for anyone looking to improve their nutrition and achieve their health and wellness goals. Whether you're new to meal planning or looking to improve your current eating habits, a well-planned meal plan can help to achieve optimal health and wellness.

A balanced meal plan should include a variety of foods from all food groups, in the appropriate portions. This includes: Fruits and vegetables: These foods are high in fiber, vitamins, and minerals, and are important for maintaining good health. Aim to include at least 5 servings of fruits and vegetables in your daily meal plan.

Whole grains: Whole grain bread, cereal, pasta, and rice provide complex carbohydrates, fiber, and other important nutrients. Make at least half of the grains you eat each day from whole grains.

Lean protein: Foods such as chicken, fish, beans, and tofu provide the body with essential amino acids and help to build and repair tissues. A serving of lean protein should be consumed with every meal.

Low-fat dairy products: Yogurt, cheese, and milk are all excellent sources of calcium and other necessary nutrients. Choose low-fat options to keep calorie intake in check.

Healthy fats: Foods such as nuts, seeds, and avocado are a good source of healthy monounsaturated and polyunsaturated fats, which can help to improve heart health.

It's also important to consider portion sizes when planning a meal.

A serving size of protein is about the size of a deck of cards, while a serving of carbohydrates is about the size of a tennis ball. A registered dietitian can provide guidance on portion sizes and recommend the appropriate number of servings for each food group, based on individual calorie needs and goals.

Incorporating healthy snacks into your meal plan is also important. Snacks can help to keep you full and satisfied between meals and can also provide important nutrients. Some healthy snack options include fruit, yogurt, nuts, and whole grain crackers.

Finally, it's important to be mindful of calorie-dense foods, such as sugar-sweetened drinks, baked goods, and fried foods. These foods are high in calories and low in essential nutrients and should be limited in a balanced meal plan.

In summary, a balanced meal plan is essential for achieving optimal health and wellness.

It should include a variety of foods from all food groups, in appropriate portions, and be adjusted based on individual calorie needs and goals.

Consultation with a registered dietitian can provide personalized recommendations for a balanced meal plan.

Daily meal structure

A typical daily meal structure for a 1200 calorie diet could look like this:

Breakfast (400 calories):

Whole grain cereal with low-fat milk and a sliced banana

An omelet with vegetables and a small amount of cheese

A smoothie with Greek yogurt, berries, and almond milk

Lunch (400 calories):

Grilled chicken or turkey sandwich with whole grain bread and a variety of vegetables

Lentil soup with a side salad and a whole grain roll

A quinoa and vegetable stir-fry

Snack (100 calories):

fruit, such as an apple or a pear.

A serving of raw veggies with hummus

A hard-boiled egg

Dinner (300 calories):

Grilled fish or tofu with a sweet potato and steamed or roasted vegetables.

A vegetable and bean chili with a side salad

A vegetable and cheese whole grain wrap

It is important to remember that these meal suggestions are just examples, and portion sizes may vary based on individual calorie needs and dietary restrictions. Consulting a healthcare professional or registered dietitian can help determine the best meal plan for your individual needs.

Recipes for each meal

Here are some recipes that fit within the calorie limits of a 1200 calorie meal plan:

Breakfast (400 calories):

Sliced banana and whole-grain cereal with low-fat milk:

1 cup of whole grain cereal

1 cup of low-fat milk

1 medium banana, sliced

Optional: 1 tsp of honey or maple syrup for added sweetness

Veggie and Cheese Omelet:

2 large eggs

vegetables, such as bell peppers, onions, and mushrooms, in the amount of 1/4 cup

1 oz of shredded cheese

Salt and pepper to taste

Optional: whole grain toast on the side

Berry and Yogurt Smoothie:

1 cup of mixed berries

1 cup of Greek yogurt

1/2 cup of almond milk

Optional: 1 tsp of honey or maple syrup for added sweetness

Lunch (400 calories):

Grilled Chicken or Turkey Sandwich:

2 slices of whole grain bread

3 oz of grilled chicken or turkey breast

1 slice of cheese

Lettuce, tomato, and avocado slices

Optional: mustard or low-fat mayonnaise

Lentil Soup with Side Salad and Whole Grain Roll:

1 cup of lentil soup

1 large green salad with mixed greens, vegetables, and a vinaigrette dressing

1 whole grain roll

Quinoa and Vegetable Stir-Fry:

1 cup of cooked quinoa

1 cup of mixed vegetables, such as broccoli, carrots, and bell peppers

3 oz of grilled chicken or tofu

1 tbsp of low-sodium soy sauce

Optional: 1 tsp of sesame oil for added flavor

Snack (100 calories):

Apple slices with Almond Butter:

1 medium apple, sliced

1 tbsp of almond butter

Raw Veggies with Hummus:

1 cup of mixed raw veggies, such as carrots, cucumbers, and bell peppers

2 tbsp of hummus

Hard-Boiled Egg:

1 large hard-boiled egg

Dinner (300 calories):

Grilled Fish or Tofu with Sweet Potato and Steamed or Roasted Vegetables:

4 oz of grilled fish or tofu

1 medium sweet potato, roasted or steamed

1 cup of steamed or roasted vegetables, such as broccoli, carrots, and green beans

Optional: 1 tsp of olive oil and lemon juice for added flavor

Vegetable and Bean Chili with Side Salad:

1 cup of vegetable and bean chili

1 large green salad with mixed greens, vegetables, and a vinaigrette dressing

Vegetable and Cheese Whole Grain Wrap:

1 whole grain wrap

1/4 cup of shredded cheese

1 cup of mixed raw or roasted vegetables, such as bell peppers, lettuce, and tomato

Optional: 1 tbsp of low-fat mayonnaise or hummus

These are just some examples of delicious and nutritious meals that fit within the calorie limits of a 1200 calorie diet. As always, it's best to consult a healthcare professional or registered dietitian to determine the best meal plan for your individual needs and goals.

Nutritional information for each meal

Here's the approximate nutritional information for each of the meals in a 1200 calorie diet:

Breakfast (400 calories):

Low-fat milk, sliced bananas, and whole grain cereal::

Total Calories: 400

Protein: 14 g

Carbohydrates: 76 g

Fat: 7 g

Veggie and Cheese Omelet:

Total Calories: 400

Protein: 28 g

Carbohydrates: 8 g

Fat: 27 g

Berry and Yogurt Smoothie:

Total Calories: 400

Protein: 27 g

Carbohydrates: 44 g

Fat: 13 g

Lunch (400 calories):

Grilled Chicken or Turkey Sandwich:

Total Calories: 400

Protein: 40 g

Carbohydrates: 45 g

Fat: 11 g

Lentil Soup with Side Salad and Whole Grain Roll:

Total Calories: 400

Protein: 20 g

Carbohydrates: 60 g

Fat: 10 g

Quinoa and Vegetable Stir-Fry:

Total Calories: 400

Protein: 30 g

Carbohydrates: 55 g

Fat: 10 g

Snack (100 calories):

Apple slices with Almond Butter:

Total Calories: 100

Protein: 2 g

Carbohydrates: 14 g

Fat: 7 g

Raw Veggies with Hummus:

Total Calories: 100

Protein: 4 g

Carbohydrates: 14 g

Fat: 4 g

Hard-Boiled Egg:

Total Calories: 100

Protein: 7 g

Carbohydrates: 1 g

Fat: 7 g

Dinner (300 calories):

Grilled Fish or Tofu with Sweet Potato and Steamed or Roasted Vegetables:

Total Calories: 300

Protein: 25 g

Carbohydrates: 36 g

Fat: 8 g

Vegetable and Bean Chili with Side Salad:

Total Calories: 300

Protein: 20 g

Carbohydrates: 42 g

Fat: 8 g

Vegetable and Cheese Whole Grain Wrap:

Total Calories: 300

Protein: 20 g

Carbohydrates: 36 g

Fat: 10 g

Please note that these nutritional values are approximate and may vary based on portion size and specific ingredients used. For individualized advice, it is always best to speak with a registered dietitian or other healthcare provider.

CHAPTER FOUR

Breakfast

Here are some healthy and delicious breakfast options for a 1200 calorie diet:

Sliced banana and whole-grain cereal with low-fat milk:

Total Calories: 400

Protein: 14 g

Carbohydrates: 76 g

Fat: 7 g

Veggie and Cheese Omelet:

Total Calories: 400

Protein: 28 g

Carbohydrates: 8 g

Fat: 27 g

Berry and Yogurt Smoothie:

Total Calories: 400

Protein: 27 g

Carbohydrates: 44 g

Fat: 13 g

Banana slices and peanut butter on whole-wheat toast:

Total Calories: 400

Protein: 16 g

Carbohydrates: 54 g

Fat: 19 g

Oatmeal with Nuts, Berries, and Low-Fat Milk:

Total Calories: 400

Protein: 21 g

Carbohydrates: 68 g

Fat: 11 g

Please note that these nutritional values are approximate and may vary based on portion size and specific ingredients used. For individualized advice, it is always best to speak with a registered dietitian or other healthcare provider.

Sample breakfast options

Here are some healthy and delicious breakfast options for a 1200 calorie diet:

Sliced banana and whole-grain cereal with low-fat milk:

Total Calories: 400

Protein: 14 g

Carbohydrates: 76 g

Fat: 7 g

Veggie and Cheese Omelet:

Total Calories: 400

Protein: 28 g

Carbohydrates: 8 g

Fat: 27 g

Berry and Yogurt Smoothie:

Total Calories: 400

Protein: 27 g

Carbohydrates: 44 g

Fat: 13 g

Sliced banana and whole-grain toast with peanut butter:

Total Calories: 400

Protein: 16 g

Carbohydrates: 54 g

Fat: 19 g

Oatmeal with Nuts, Berries, and Low-Fat Milk:

Total Calories: 400

Protein: 21 g

Carbohydrates: 68 g

Fat: 11 g

Please note that these nutritional values are approximate and may vary based on portion size and specific ingredients used. For individualized advice, it is always best to speak with a registered dietitian or other healthcare provider.

CHAPTER FIVE

Recipe for each breakfast

Sliced banana and whole-grain cereal with low-fat milk.

Here is a simple method to prepare Whole Grain Cereal with Low-Fat Milk and Sliced Banana:

Ingredients:

1 cup of whole grain cereal

1 cup of low-fat milk

1 medium banana, sliced.

Instructions:

Pour cereal into a bowl.

Pour milk over the cereal and let it sit for a minute or two to soften the cereal.

Top with sliced bananas.

Serve immediately and enjoy!

Note: You can also add a tablespoon of honey, a handful of berries or a sprinkle of cinnamon for added flavor.

The type of cereal you choose will affect the nutritional values, so be sure to check the label for details.

Veggie and Cheese Omelet

Here is a simple method to prepare a Veggie and Cheese Omelet:

Ingredients:

2 large eggs

2 tablespoons of milk

Salt and pepper, to taste

1 tablespoon of oil or butter

1/2 cup of diced vegetables (such as bell peppers, onions, and mushrooms)

1/4 cup of shredded cheese (such as cheddar or Monterey jack)

Instructions:

In a medium bowl, combine the eggs, milk, salt, and pepper.

In a sizable nonstick skillet over medium heat, melt butter or oil.

Add the diced vegetables to the skillet and cook until they are soft and tender, about 5 minutes.

Pour the egg mixture over the vegetables and let it cook until the bottom is set, about 2-3 minutes.

Sprinkle the cheese over one half of the omelet.

Using a spatula, carefully fold the other half of the omelet over the cheese, so that it covers the cheese.

Cook for an additional minute, until the cheese is melted, and the egg is fully cooked.

The omelet should be placed hot on a plate.

Note: You can also add ham, bacon or sausage to this omelet for added flavor and protein. You can also use a variety of different vegetables or cheese to suit your taste preferences.

Berry and Yogurt Smoothie

Here is a simple method to prepare a Berry and Yogurt Smoothie:

Ingredients:

1 cup of frozen mixed berries (such as strawberries, blueberries, and raspberries)

1 cup of low-fat yogurt

1/2 cup of orange juice

1 scoop of protein powder (optional)

1 teaspoon of honey (optional)

Instructions:

Place all ingredients in a blender.

Blend until smooth and creamy.

Pour into a glass and enjoy immediately.

Note: You can use any type of frozen or fresh berries, and any type of yogurt that you prefer. If you want a sweeter smoothie, you can add more honey or a natural sweetener of your choice. If you want to increase the protein content, you can add a scoop of protein powder. Experiment with different ingredients and ratios to find your perfect smoothie combination.

Sliced banana and whole-grain toast with peanut butter.

Here is a simple method to prepare Whole Grain Toast with Peanut Butter and Sliced Banana:

Ingredients:

2 slices of whole grain bread

2 tablespoons of peanut butter

1 medium banana, sliced.

Instructions:

Toast the whole grain bread until it is golden brown and crispy.

Each slice of toast should have 1 tablespoon of peanut butter on it.

Top each slice of toast with sliced bananas.

Serve immediately and enjoy!

Note: You can also add a drizzle of honey, a sprinkle of cinnamon or a handful of berries for added flavor. You can also use almond butter, cashew butter or any other nut butter of your choice instead of peanut butter.

Oatmeal with Nuts, Berries, and Low-Fat Milk

Here is a simple method to prepare Oatmeal with Nuts, Berries, and Low-Fat Milk:

Ingredients:

1/2 cup of rolled oats.

1 cup of water or low-fat milk

1/4 cup of mixed berries (such as strawberries, blueberries, and raspberries)

1 tablespoon of chopped nuts (such as almonds, walnuts, or pecans)

1 teaspoon of honey (optional)

Instructions:

In a medium saucepan, heat the water or milk to a rolling boil.

Stir in the rolled oats and reduce heat to low.

Cook for about 5 minutes, stirring occasionally, or until the oatmeal is thick and creamy.

Stir in the mixed berries, chopped nuts, and honey (if using).

Serve immediately and enjoy!

Note: You can also add a drizzle of maple syrup, a sprinkle of cinnamon or a spoonful of peanut butter for added flavor. You can also use any type of nuts, berries or sweetener that you prefer. Try experimenting with different ingredients to find your perfect oatmeal combination!

Nutritional information for each breakfast

Sliced banana and whole-grain cereal with low-fat milk nutritional information.

The nutritional information for 1 serving of Whole Grain Cereal with Low-Fat Milk and Sliced Banana is as follows (assuming a serving size of 1 cup of cereal, 1 cup of low-fat milk, and 1 medium banana):

Calories: Approximately 375

Protein: Approximately 14g

Fat: Approximately 5g

Saturated Fat: Approximately 2g

Carbohydrates: Approximately 73g

Fiber: Approximately 8g

Sugar: Approximately 32g

Sodium: Approximately 222mg

This meal is a good source of protein, fiber, vitamins, and minerals, and provides a balanced mix of carbohydrates and healthy fats to help you start your day with sustained energy. Keep in mind that the exact nutritional information may vary depending on the specific brands and ingredients used.

Veggie and Cheese Omelet nutritional information

The nutritional information for 1 serving of Veggie and Cheese Omelet (assuming 2 eggs, 1/4 cup each of chopped bell peppers and onions, and 2 tablespoons of shredded cheddar cheese) is as follows:

Calories: Approximately 250

Protein: Approximately 20g

Fat: Approximately 18g

Saturated Fat: Approximately 7g

Carbohydrates: Approximately 5g

Fiber: Approximately 1g

Sugar: Approximately 2g

Sodium: Approximately 450mg

This meal is a good source of protein, healthy fats, and vitamins and minerals, especially vitamin A and C from the veggies. It provides a good balance of nutrients to keep you full and energized throughout the morning. The exact nutritional information may vary depending on the specific brands and ingredients used.

Berry and Yogurt Smoothie nutritional information

The nutritional information for 1 serving of Berry and Yogurt Smoothie (assuming 1 cup of mixed berries, 1 cup of low-fat Greek yogurt, and 1/2 cup of almond milk) is as follows:

Calories: Approximately 250

Protein: Approximately 20g

Fat: Approximately 5g

Saturated Fat: Approximately 1g

Carbohydrates: Approximately 35g

Fiber: Approximately 5g

Sugar: Approximately 25g

Sodium: Approximately 125mg

This meal is a good source of protein, fiber, vitamins, and minerals, and provides a good balance of carbohydrates and healthy fats to help you start your day with sustained energy. The exact nutritional information may vary depending on the specific brands and ingredients used.

Whole Grain Toast with Peanut Butter and Sliced Banana nutritional information

Whole Grain Toast with Peanut Butter and Sliced Banana nutritional information:

The nutritional information for 1 serving of Whole Grain Toast with Peanut Butter and Sliced Banana (assuming 2 slices of whole grain toast, 2 tablespoons of peanut butter, and 1 medium banana) is as follows:

Calories: Approximately 500

Protein: Approximately 20g

Fat: Approximately 25g

Saturated Fat: Approximately 4g

Carbohydrates: Approximately 67g

Fiber: Approximately 9g

Sugar: Approximately 25g

Sodium: Approximately 340 mg

This meal is a good source of protein, fiber, and healthy fats, and provides a balanced mix of carbohydrates and healthy fats to help you start your day with sustained energy. Keep in mind that the exact nutritional information may vary depending on the specific brands and ingredients used.

Oatmeal with Nuts, Berries, and Low-Fat Milk nutritional information

The nutritional information for 1 serving of Oatmeal with Nuts, Berries, and Low-Fat Milk (assuming 1 cup of oats, 1/4 cup each of mixed nuts and mixed berries, and 1 cup of low-fat milk) is as follows:

Calories: Approximately 400

Protein: Approximately 16g

Fat: Approximately 20g

Saturated Fat: Approximately 3g

Carbohydrates: Approximately 40g

Fiber: Approximately 5g

Sugar: Approximately 10g

Sodium: Approximately 125mg

This meal is a good source of fiber, protein, vitamins, and minerals, and provides a good balance of healthy fats and carbohydrates to keep you full and energized throughout the morning. The exact nutritional information may vary depending on the specific brands and ingredients used.

CHAPTER SIX

Lunch

Here are some sample lunch options for a 1200 calorie diet:

Grilled Chicken Salad:

Grilled chicken breast (3-4 oz), mixed greens, cherry tomatoes, cucumber, and red onion, dressed with balsamic vinaigrette (2 tbsp).

Turkey and Avocado Wrap:

Whole grain wrap, turkey breast slices (3-4 oz), mashed avocado, lettuce, and tomato slices.

Veggie and Hummus Wrap:

Whole grain wrap, hummus, mixed veggies (e.g. carrots, cucumber, bell peppers), and feta cheese.

Tuna Salad Sandwich:

Whole grain bread, tuna in water (drained), light mayonnaise, chopped celery, and red onion.
Lentil Soup and Whole Grain Bread: Lentil soup, whole grain bread (1-2 slices).

These are just examples and can be adjusted to your personal taste preferences. Try to include a good balance of protein, healthy fats, and carbohydrates in your lunch to help you stay full and satisfied until dinner.

lunch

Here is a sample lunch for a 1200 calorie diet:

Grilled Chicken Salad:

INGREDIENTS:
Grilled chicken breast (3-4 oz)
Mixed greens

Cherry tomatoes

Cucumber

Red onion

Balsamic vinaigrette (2 tbsp)

Preparation:

Cook the chicken breast until fully cooked and let it cool.

In a large bowl, mix the greens, cherry tomatoes, cucumber, and red onion.

Slice the chicken breast and add it to the salad.

Dress the salad with balsamic vinaigrette to taste.

Serve and enjoy!

This meal provides a good balance of protein, fiber, and healthy fats, as well as essential vitamins and minerals from the greens and vegetables. The balsamic vinaigrette adds flavor while keeping the calorie count low.

Turkey and Avocado Wrap:

Ingredients:

1 whole grain wrap

3-4 oz turkey breast slices

1/2 avocado, mashed

2-3 lettuce leaves

2-3 tomato slices

Instructions:

Warm the wrap in a pan or oven for a minute or two until soft.

Spread the mashed avocado evenly over the wrap.

Place the turkey slices, lettuce leaves, and tomato slices on top of the avocado.

Roll up the wrap tightly and slice in half.

This wrap provides a good balance of protein, healthy fats, and carbohydrates, and can be a tasty and filling option for lunch.

Veggie wrap:

A veggie wrap can be a healthy and satisfying lunch option for a 1200 calorie diet. To make a veggie wrap, you'll need:

Ingredients:

1 whole grain wrap

Roasted vegetables, such as zucchini, eggplant, and red peppers

2 tablespoons of hummus

A sprinkle of feta cheese

Instructions:

Warm the wrap in a pan or on a griddle for about 30 seconds on each side.

Spread the hummus evenly on the wrap.

Place the roasted vegetables on top of the hummus.

Sprinkle the feta cheese over the vegetables.

Slice the wrap in half after tightly rolling it up.

Enjoy your delicious and nutritious veggie wrap!

Lentil soup:

Lentil soup is a great option for a healthy and filling lunch, especially if you are following a 1200 calorie diet. Here is a straightforward lentil soup recipe:

Ingredients:

1 cup of dried green lentils

1 diced onion

2 cloves of minced garlic

2 diced carrots

2 diced celery stalks

1 diced potato

4 cups of low-sodium vegetable broth

1 can of diced tomatoes

1 teaspoon of dried thyme

1 teaspoon of dried basil

Salt and pepper, to taste

Instructions:

The lentils should be rinsed in cold water and set aside.

One tablespoon of olive oil should be heated in a big pot over medium heat For three to five minutes, add the onion and garlic and cook until soft.

Add the carrots, celery, and potato and cook for another 5 minutes.

Add the lentils, vegetable broth, diced tomatoes, thyme, basil, salt, and pepper to the pot.

Bring the mixture to a boil, then reduce the heat and let it simmer for about 25-30 minutes, or until the lentils are soft.

Use an immersion blender to blend the soup until it reaches the desired consistency or transfer it in batches to a blender or food processor and blend until smooth.
Serve hot and enjoy!

This recipe makes about 6 servings and each serving is approximately 200 calories. You can also add extra veggies or spices to customize the soup to your liking.

Recipes for each lunch

Grilled chicken salad recipe

Grilled chicken salad is a nutritious and satisfying lunch option for a 1200 calorie diet.

Grilled chicken salad recipe that's easy to follow:

Ingredients:

4 ounces of boneless, skinless chicken breast

Salt and pepper, to taste

Salad greens

1 cup of chopped vegetables, such as cherry tomatoes, cucumbers, bell peppers, and red onion

1 tablespoon of a light vinaigrette dressing

Instructions:

Before cooking, season the chicken breast with salt and pepper.

Obtain medium-high heat in a grill pan or outdoor grill.

Place the chicken on the grill and cook for about 4-5 minutes on each side, or until the internal temperature reaches 165°F.

Remove the chicken from the grill and let it rest for 5 minutes.

While the chicken is resting, arrange the salad greens on a plate.

Top the greens with the chopped vegetables.

Slice the grilled chicken into thin strips and place it on top of the vegetables.

Drizzle the vinaigrette dressing over the salad.

Enjoy your delicious and nutritious grilled chicken salad! You can also switch up the vegetables and dressing to your liking.

Turkey and Avocado Wrap recipe

Here's a recipe for a delicious and healthy turkey and avocado wrap:

Ingredients:

2 whole grain tortillas

4 ounces of deli turkey breast

2 slices of tomato

2 leaves of lettuce

1/2 avocado, mashed.

1 teaspoon of Dijon mustard

Salt and pepper, to taste

Instructions:

Lay out the two tortillas on a flat surface.

Spread the mashed avocado evenly over the tortillas.

On top of the avocado, arrange the turkey slices.

Add the slices of tomato and lettuce leaves on top of the turkey.

Spread the Dijon mustard over the ingredients.
Sprinkle salt and pepper over the ingredients.
Roll up the tortillas tightly, tucking in the sides as you roll.
Cut the wraps in half and serve.

This wrap is a tasty and nutritious lunch option, with each wrap providing approximately 400 calories. You can also add other ingredients such as cheese, hot sauce, or pickles to taste. Enjoy!

Veggie wrap recipe.

Here is a recipe for a delicious and healthy veggie wrap:
Ingredients:
2 whole grain tortillas
1/2 cup of hummus

1 cup of mixed chopped vegetables, such as bell peppers, cucumber, red onion, and spinach

2 ounces of crumbled feta cheese

Salt and pepper, to taste

Instructions:

Lay out the two tortillas on a flat surface.

Spread the hummus evenly over the tortillas.

Place the chopped vegetables on top of the hummus.

Over the vegetables, strew feta cheese crumbles.

Sprinkle salt and pepper over the ingredients.

Roll up the tortillas tightly, tucking in the sides as you roll.

Cut the wraps in half and serve.

This wrap is a tasty and nutritious lunch option, with each wrap providing approximately 400 calories. You can also add other ingredients such as cheese, hot sauce, or pickles to taste. Enjoy!

Lentil soup:

Lentil soup is a nutritious and filling lunch option, especially if you're following a 1200 calorie diet. Here's a simple recipe for lentil soup:

Ingredients:

1 cup of dried green lentils

1 diced onion

2 cloves of minced garlic

2 diced carrots

2 diced celery stalks

1 diced potato

4 cups of low-sodium vegetable broth

1 can of diced tomatoes

1 teaspoon of dried thyme

1 teaspoon of dried basil

Salt and pepper, to taste

Instructions:

The lentils should be rinsed in cold water and set aside.

One tablespoon of olive oil should be heated in a big pot over medium heat. When the onion and garlic are added, cook them for 3 to 5 minutes, or until they are soft.

Add the carrots, celery, and potato and cook for another 5 minutes.

Add the lentils, vegetable broth, diced tomatoes, thyme, basil, salt, and pepper to the pot.

Bring the mixture to a boil, then reduce the heat and let it simmer for about 25-30 minutes, or until the lentils are soft.

Use an immersion blender to blend the soup until it reaches the desired consistency or transfer it in batches to a blender or food processor and blend until smooth.

Serve hot and enjoy!

This recipe makes about 6 servings and each serving is approximately 200 calories. You can also add extra veggies or spices to customize the soup to your liking. Enjoy!

Nutritional information for each lunch

Grilled chicken salad:

A serving of grilled chicken salad made from the recipe I provided would contain approximately:

400 calories

26 grams of protein

27 grams of carbohydrates

18 grams of fat

4 grams of fiber

Keep in mind that the exact nutritional information may vary depending on the specific ingredients used, such as the size and type of chicken breast, the type of dressing, and the amounts of salt and pepper used. It's always a good idea to measure your ingredients and use a food scale to ensure accuracy when tracking your calorie intake.

Turkey wraps nutritional information:

A serving of turkey and avocado wrap made from the recipe I provided would contain approximately:

400 calories

30 grams of protein

40 grams of carbohydrates

15 grams of fat

6 grams of fiber

Keep in mind that the exact nutritional information may vary depending on the specific ingredients used, such as the size of the tortilla, the amount of avocado, and the amount of Dijon mustard used. It's always a good idea to measure your ingredients and use a food scale to ensure accuracy when tracking your calorie intake.

Veggie wrap nutritional information:

A serving of veggie wrap made from the recipe I provided would contain approximately:

400 calories

14 grams of protein

52 grams of carbohydrates

16 grams of fat

12 grams of fiber

Keep in mind that the exact nutritional information may vary depending on the specific ingredients used, such as the size of the tortilla, the type of hummus, and the amount of feta cheese used. It's always a good idea to measure your ingredients and use a food scale to ensure accuracy when tracking your calorie intake.

Lentil soup nutritional information:

A serving of lentil soup made from the recipe I provided would contain approximately:

200 calories

12 grams of protein

32 grams of carbohydrates

2 grams of fat

10 grams of fiber

Keep in mind that the exact nutritional information may vary depending on the specific ingredients used, such as the type of lentils, the amount of salt and pepper used, and the type of broth. It's always a good idea to measure your ingredients and use a food scale to ensure accuracy when tracking your calorie intake.

CHAPTER SEVEN

Dinner

If you're following a 1200 calorie diet, here are some healthy dinner options that you might find helpful:

Grilled chicken or fish with roasted vegetables

Salad with grilled tofu or shrimp

Lentil or vegetable stir-fry with brown rice

black beans, salsa, and baked sweet potatoes

Quinoa or vegetable chili

Grilled chicken or veggie kabobs with a mixed greens salad

Brown rice and roasted asparagus with baked salmon

When planning your meals, aim for a balanced plate with a serving of protein, whole grains, and vegetables. You can also season your food with herbs and spices for flavor, and use healthy fats such as olive oil in cooking.

dinner options

Here are some sample dinner options for a 1200 calorie diet:

Salmon grilled over coals, served with roasted vegetables and a quinoa salad.

Chicken stir-fry with brown rice and steamed broccoli.

a mixed greens salad, whole grain crackers, and lentil soup.

Baked sweet potato topped with black beans, salsa, and a side of steamed spinach.

Grilled chicken or tofu kebabs with mixed vegetables and a side of brown rice.

Vegetable omelet with a mixed greens salad and whole grain toast.

Whole grain pasta with a tomato-based vegetable sauce and a side of roasted Brussels sprouts.

Remember to balance your plate with a serving of protein, whole grains, and vegetables. You can also season your food with herbs and spices for flavor and use healthy fats such as olive oil in cooking.

Recipes for each dinner

Grilled Salmon with Roasted Vegetables and Quinoa Salad Recipe:

Ingredients:

4 salmon fillets (4 oz each)

1 tbsp olive oil

Salt and pepper to taste.

1 lb. mixed vegetables (such as bell peppers, zucchini, and cherry tomatoes)

1 cup uncooked quinoa

2 cups water

2 tbsp lemon juice

1 tbsp balsamic vinegar

1 clove garlic, minced

1 tbsp Dijon mustard

2 tbsp extra-virgin olive oil

Add pepper and salt to taste when seasoning.

Instructions:

Preheat your grill or oven to 400°F.

Place the salmon fillets in a baking dish and brush with 1 tbsp olive oil. Season with salt and pepper to taste.

Place the mixed vegetables on a baking sheet and toss with 1 tbsp olive oil. Add pepper and salt to taste when seasoning. Roast in the oven or grill for 15-20 minutes, or until the vegetables are tender and the salmon is cooked through.

Rinse the quinoa in a fine-mesh strainer and place it in a medium saucepan with 2 cups of water. Bring to a boil, then reduce the heat to low and simmer for 15-20 minutes, or until the quinoa is tender and the water is absorbed.

In a large bowl, whisk together the lemon juice, balsamic vinegar, garlic, Dijon mustard, 2 tbsp olive oil, salt, and pepper. Add the cooked quinoa and roasted vegetables and toss to combine.

Serve the grilled salmon with the quinoa salad on the side. Enjoy!

Chicken Stir-Fry with Brown Rice and Steamed Broccoli Recipe:

Ingredients:

Chicken breasts weighing one pound, thinly sliced, and skinless.

2 cups brown rice

4 cups water

1 head of broccoli, cut into florets.

1 tbsp olive oil

2 cloves garlic, minced.

1 tbsp grated ginger

1 red bell pepper, sliced.

1 yellow onion, sliced.

2 tbsp soy sauce

1 tbsp honey

1 tbsp cornstarch

2 tbsp water

Salt and pepper to taste

Instructions:

Cook the brown rice according to package instructions in 4 cups of water.

In a large saucepan, bring 1 inch of water to a boil and place a steamer basket inside. Place the broccoli florets in the basket, cover the saucepan, and steam for 5-7 minutes, or until the broccoli is tender.

In a large wok or skillet, heat 1 tbsp olive oil over high heat. Add the chicken strips and stir-fry for 2-3 minutes, or until browned.Chicken .

In the same wok, add the garlic, ginger, red bell pepper, and onion. until the vegetables are tender, stir-fry for 2 to 3 minutes.

In a small bowl, whisk together the soy sauce, honey, cornstarch, and 2 tbsp water. Add the chicken back to the wok and pour the sauce over the chicken and vegetables. until the sauce has thickened, stir-fry for 2 to 3 minutes.

Serve the chicken stir-fry over a bed of cooked brown rice, with the steamed broccoli on the side. Enjoy!

Lentil or Vegetable Stir-Fry with Brown Rice Recipe:

Ingredients:

1 cup brown rice

2 cups water

1 cup cooked green or brown lentils.

1 tbsp olive oil

2 cloves garlic, minced.

1 tbsp grated ginger

2 cups mixed vegetables (such as bell peppers, zucchini, carrots, and snow peas)

2 tbsp soy sauce

1 tbsp rice vinegar

1 tsp sesame oil

Salt and pepper to taste

Instructions:

Cook the brown rice according to package instructions in 2 cups of water.

In a large wok or skillet, heat 1 tbsp olive oil over high heat.

Add the garlic, ginger, mixed vegetables, and cooked lentils until the vegetables are tender, stir-fry for 2 to 3 minutes.

Combine the soy sauce, rice vinegar, sesame oil, salt, and pepper in a small bowl. Pour the sauce over the vegetable and lentil mixture and stir-fry for an additional 2-3 minutes, or until the sauce has thickened.

Serve the vegetable and lentil stir-fry over a bed of cooked brown rice. Enjoy!

Baked Sweet Potato with Black Beans and Salsa Recipe:

Ingredients:

4 medium sweet potatoes

Draining and rinsing one can of black beans

1/2 cup salsa

2 tbsp olive oil

Salt and pepper to taste

Optional toppings: shredded cheese, cilantro, avocado, and sour cream

Instructions:

Preheat the oven to 400°F (200°C).

Wash and pierce the sweet potatoes several times with a fork. Place them on a baking sheet lined with parchment paper and bake for 45-50 minutes, or until tender.

The black beans should be heated in a small pan over medium heat. Stir in the salsa and season with salt and pepper to taste.

When the sweet potatoes are done, slice them open lengthwise and top with the black bean and salsa mixture. Drizzle with olive oil and any additional toppings of your choice. Enjoy!

Here is a simple recipe for a vegetable quinoa chili:

Ingredients:

1 tablespoon olive oil

1 medium onion, chopped.

3 cloves garlic, minced.

1 red bell pepper, chopped.

1 yellow squash, chopped.

1 zucchini, chopped.

1 can (14.5 ounces) diced tomatoes.

2 cups vegetable broth

1 can (15 ounces) dark beans depleted and flushed.

kidney beans, drained and rinsed, from a single 15-ounce can.

1 teaspoon chili powder

1 teaspoon ground cumin

1/2 teaspoon dried oregano

Salt and black pepper to taste.

1 cup quinoa, rinsed.

Sharp cream and crumbled cheddar for decoration (discretionary)

Instructions:

Warm the oil over medium-low heat in a big pot or Dutch oven. 5 minutes should be enough time to soften the onion and garlic after adding them.

Add the bell pepper, yellow squash, zucchini, diced tomatoes, vegetable broth, black beans, kidney beans, chili powder, cumin, oregano, salt, and pepper. Boil for a few minutes, then turn down the heat and simmer for 20.

Stir in the quinoa, cover and cook until the quinoa is tender and the liquid is absorbed, about 20 minutes.

Serve with shredded cheese and a dollop of sour cream, if desired. Enjoy!

Here is a simple recipe for grilled chicken or veggie kabobs with a mixed greens salad:

Kabobs:

1-pound boneless, skinless chicken breast or firm tofu, cut into 1 1/2 inch pieces

a single red onion, diced into 1 1/2 inch pieces

a single red bell pepper, diced into 1 1/2 inch pieces

Cut one yellow bell pepper into 1 1/2-inch pieces.

1 zucchini, cut into 1/2 inch rounds

Cut one yellow squash into 1/2-inch rounds.

2 tablespoons olive oil

2 tablespoons balsamic vinegar

1 tablespoon dried oregano

1 tablespoon dried basil

Salt and black pepper to taste

Kebabs (whether using wooden skewers, soak those in water for thirty minutes before using)

Mixed Greens Salad:

6 cups mixed greens

1 large carrot, grated

1 large red apple, diced

1/2 cup raisins

1/2 cup walnuts, chopped.

2 tablespoons red wine vinegar

1 tablespoon Dijon mustard

2 tablespoons olive oil

Salt and black pepper to taste

Instructions:

Preheat grill to medium-high heat.

In a large bowl, whisk together the olive oil, balsamic vinegar, oregano, basil, salt, and pepper. Add the chicken or tofu and vegetables to the bowl and toss to coat.

Alternately thread the chicken or tofu and vegetables onto the skewers.

Grill the kabobs for 10-15 minutes, turning occasionally, until the chicken is cooked through or the tofu is golden brown.

In a large bowl, combine the mixed greens, carrot, apple, raisins, and walnuts.

In a small bowl, whisk together the red wine vinegar, Dijon mustard, olive oil, salt, and pepper.

Toss the salad with the dressing after drizzling it over it. Serve alongside the grilled kabobs. Enjoy!

Here's a simple recipe for baked salmon with roasted asparagus and brown rice:

Ingredients:

4 salmon fillets

1 lb asparagus

1 cup brown rice

2 tablespoons olive oil

Salt and pepper to taste

Lemon wedges (optional)

Instructions:

Preheat oven to 400°F.

Rinse the brown rice and add it to a pot with 2 cups of water.

. After bringing to a boil, turn down the heat, cover the pot, and simmer for 35–40 minutes.

While the rice is cooking, prepare the asparagus by cutting off the tough bottom ends and tossing with 1 tablespoon of olive oil and salt and pepper to taste.

Place the asparagus on a baking sheet and roast in the oven for 15-20 minutes.

In a separate baking dish, place the salmon fillets and brush with the remaining 1 tablespoon of olive oil. As desired, season with salt and pepper..

When the asparagus is done, remove from oven and place the salmon in the oven on a separate rack. Salmon should be baked for 12 to 15 minutes, or until it flakes easily.

Serve the salmon over a bed of cooked brown rice and with the roasted asparagus on the side. Squeeze lemon wedges over the salmon before serving, if desired. Enjoy!

Nutritional information for each dinner

Grilled chicken or fish with roasted vegetables

The nutritional information of grilled chicken or fish with roasted vegetables depends on several factors, such as the type of fish or chicken, the method of cooking, the size of the portion, and the type of vegetables used.

However, generally speaking, grilled chicken breast is a lean protein source that contains about 165 calories, 3 grams of fat, and 31 grams of protein per 3.5 ounces (100 grams).

Fish is also a good source of protein and omega-3 fatty acids, and the calorie and fat content will vary depending on the type of fish. For example, a 3.5-ounce (100-gram) serving of salmon provides about 175 calories, 11 grams of fat, and 22 grams of protein.

Roasted vegetables are a healthy and low-calorie addition to a meal, with a typical serving of roasted vegetables containing about 50-100 calories, depending on the type of vegetables and the method of preparation.

It's important to keep in mind that the calorie and nutrient content can vary greatly depending on the cooking methods used and the type and amount of added ingredients, such as oil, spices, and sauces.

Salad with grilled tofu or shrimp
Grilled Tofu Salad:

Serving size: 1 bowl (about 300 g)

Calories: 380

Fat: 15 g

Saturated Fat: 2 g

Cholesterol: 0 mg

Sodium: 590 mg

Total Carbohydrates: 37 g

Dietary Fiber: 7 g

Sugars: 5 g

Protein: 25 g

Grilled Shrimp Salad:

Serving size: 1 bowl (about 300 g)

Calories: 360

Fat: 15 g

Saturated Fat: 2 g

Cholesterol: 170 mg

Sodium: 660 mg

Total Carbohydrates: 37 g

Dietary Fiber: 7 g

Sugars: 5 g

Protein: 29 g

Note: These values may vary depending on the ingredients used and the portion size.

Lentil or vegetable stir-fry with brown rice

The nutritional information for a lentil or vegetable stir-fry with brown rice will vary depending on the ingredients used, but here is a rough estimate based on a 1-cup serving.

Calories: Approximately 300-400

Fat: Approximately 5-10 g

Protein: Approximately 12-20 g

Carbohydrates: Approximately 50-60 g

Fiber: Approximately 7-10 g

Sugar: Approximately 5-10 g

Sodium: Approximately 300-500 mg

Note: The above nutritional information is based on estimates and may vary based on the specific ingredients used in the stir-fry. It is always best to consult a nutritionist or consult the label on specific ingredient packages for more accurate information.

black beans, salsa, and baked sweet potatoes.

Here is a rough estimate of the nutritional information for a baked sweet potato with black beans and salsa:

Serving size: 1 medium sweet potato

Calories: approximately 300

Fat: 4 grams

Saturated Fat: 1 gram

Cholesterol: 0 milligrams

Sodium: 400 milligrams

Carbohydrates: 60 grams

Fiber: 9 grams

Sugar: 10 grams

Protein: 10 grams

Note: The nutritional information may vary based on the ingredients used and the portion size. This estimate is based on using 1 medium baked sweet potato, 1/2 cup black beans, and 1/4 cup salsa.

Quinoa or vegetable chili

Quinoa Chili:

Serving size: 1 cup (237 g)

Calories: 254

Protein: 8.14 g

Fat: 7.06 g

Carbohydrates: 41.76 g

Fiber: 5.2 g

Sugar: 2.07 g

Sodium: 505 mg

Vegetable Chili:

Serving size: 1 cup (237 g)

Calories: 95

Protein: 4 g

Fat: 2 g

Carbohydrates: 16 g

Fiber: 5 g

Sugar: 5 g

Sodium: 686 mg

Note: The nutritional information can vary based on the ingredients used and serving size. These values are an estimate and should be used as a reference only.

Grilled chicken or veggie kabobs with a mixed greens salad

Grilled Chicken Kabobs (3 oz chicken per skewer):

-Calories: 150

-Fat: 4g

-Saturated Fat: 1g

-Cholesterol: 73mg

-Sodium: 68mg

-Carbohydrates: 2g

-Protein: 26g

Veggie Kabobs (1 oz vegetables per skewer):

-Calories: 46

-Fat: 1g

-Saturated Fat: 0g

-Cholesterol: 0mg

-Sodium: 16mg

-Carbohydrates: 10g

-Protein: 2g

Mixed Greens Salad (1 cup):

-Calories: 10

-Fat: 0g

-Saturated Fat: 0g

-Cholesterol: 0mg

-Sodium: 3mg

-Carbohydrates: 2g

-Protein: 1g

roasted asparagus, salmon, and brown rice in the oven
Here is an estimated nutritional information for a serving of
baked salmon with roasted asparagus and brown rice (based
on a serving size of 6 ounces of salmon, 1 cup of brown rice,
and 1 cup of asparagus):

Calories: 637

Protein: 37 g

Fat: 17 g (4 g of which are saturated)

Carbohydrates: 77 g

Fiber: 6 g

Sugar: 3 g

Sodium: 136 mg

Note: Nutritional information may vary based on the specific
ingredients used and preparation method.

CHAPTER EIGHT

Snacks

Here are some snack options for a 1200 calorie diet:

Greek yogurt with mixed berries and a drizzle of honey

Carrot sticks with hummus.

Apple slices with almond butter

Rice cake with avocado and a sprinkle of salt

Remember to balance your snacks with the rest of your daily calorie intake and choose options that are high in fiber and protein.

Healthy snack options

Here are five healthy snack options for a 1200 calorie diet:

Fresh fruit: Choose a medium-sized piece of fruit, such as an apple, orange, or banana, for a satisfying snack.

Raw veggies: Carrots, celery, cherry tomatoes, and cucumber slices are great options for a crunchy, low-calorie snack.

Yogurt: opt for a plain Greek yogurt and add some fresh berries or a drizzle of honey for flavor.

Nuts: A small handful of almonds, walnuts, or cashews provides a healthy dose of protein and healthy fats.

Rice crackers: Choose a whole grain variety and top with a smear of avocado or hummus for added flavor and nutrition.

Remember to keep portion sizes in mind and choose snacks that are high in fiber and protein to keep you feeling full and satisfied between meals.

Recipes for each snack

Fresh fruit

Here is a simple recipe for a fresh fruit salad:

Ingredients:

2 cups of berry mixture (strawberries, blueberries, raspberries, blackberries)

1 medium ripe mango, peeled and diced

1 medium kiwi, peeled and diced

1 medium banana, sliced

1/4 cup freshly squeezed orange juice

1 tbsp honey (optional)

Instructions:

Wash and prepare all the fruit.

In a large bowl, mix the mixed berries, mango, kiwi, and banana.

Orange juice and honey should be whipped together in a small bowl (if using).

Pour the orange juice mixture over the fruit salad and gently toss to combine.

Serve right away or keep chilled for a minimum of two days in an airtight container.

Enjoy your delicious and nutritious fresh fruit salad!

Raw veggies

Here is a simple and delicious recipe for raw veggies:

Crunchy Veggie Snack:

Ingredients:

2 cups of carrots, sliced.

2 cups of celery, sliced.

1 cup of cherry tomatoes, halved.

1 cup of cucumber, sliced.

1/4 cup of your favorite dip (hummus, ranch, tzatziki, etc.)

Instructions:

Wash and prepare the vegetables by slicing or halving as needed.

Arrange the veggies on a platter or in a large bowl.

Serve with your favorite dip in a small bowl for dipping.

This crunchy veggie snack is a great option for a low-calorie, high-fiber snack. You can also add other veggies, such as bell peppers or snap peas, to vary the flavors and textures.

Enjoy as both a dipping sauce with your preferred meal or as a snack.

Yogurt:

Here is a delicious and healthy yogurt recipe:

Strawberry Chia Seed Yogurt

Ingredients:

1 cup Greek yogurt

1 cup fresh strawberries, chopped

2 tbsp honey

2 tbsp chia seeds

Instructions:

Greek yogurt and honey should be thoroughly blended in a small bowl.

Stir in the chopped strawberries and chia seeds.

Put the bowl in the refrigerator overnight or for at least two hours.

Serve cold and enjoy!

This yogurt recipe is a great way to add some extra nutrients and flavor to your morning routine. You can also customize it with your favorite fruit and sweetener. Enjoy!

Nut:

Here is a healthy and delicious nut recipe:

Maple Cinnamon Roasted Almonds:

Ingredients:

1 cup raw almonds

1 tbsp pure maple syrup

1 tsp cinnamon

1/4 tsp salt

Instructions:

Preheat oven to 350°F. A baking sheet should be covered with parchment paper.

In a small bowl, whisk together the maple syrup, cinnamon, and salt.

In a separate large bowl, mix the almonds with the maple syrup mixture until the nuts are evenly coated.

On the prepared baking sheet, arrange the coated almonds in a single layer.

Bake for 10-15 minutes or until the almonds are golden brown and fragrant.

Allow the almonds to cool completely on the baking sheet.

Serve as a snack or sprinkle over oatmeal, yogurt, or salads for added crunch and flavor.

Enjoy this healthy and satisfying nut recipe!

Rice crackers:

Here is a simple recipe for homemade rice crackers:

Ingredients:

2 cups brown rice flour

2 tablespoons olive oil

1 teaspoon salt

1/2 cup warm water

Instructions:

Preheat the oven to 400°F (200°C). Put parchment paper on a baking tray.

In a large mixing bowl, combine the brown rice flour, olive oil, and salt.

Add the warm water gradually, stirring with a fork until a dough forms.

The dough should be turned out and kneaded for two to three minutes until it is smooth.

The flour should be rolled out over 1/8 thickness. Cut the dough into desired shapes, such as squares or triangles.

Place the crackers on the prepared baking sheet. The edges should be golden brown after baking for 10 to 12 minutes.

Remove from the oven and let cool completely on a wire rack. Put away for up to a week within an air - tight container.

Enjoy your homemade rice crackers as a snack, with soup or salad, or as a gluten-free alternative to traditional crackers.

Nutritional information for each snack

Fresh fruit salad

The nutritional information of a fresh fruit salad can vary depending on the specific fruits included. However, a typical serving of fresh fruit salad (around 1 cup) can provide:

Approximately 80-100 calories

1-2 grams of protein

0-1 gram of fat

20-25 grams of carbohydrates, mostly from natural sugars

2-3 grams of fiber

Vitamin C, potassium, and other vitamins and minerals, depending on the types of fruits used.

Keep in mind that added ingredients such as sugar, syrup, or cream can significantly increase the calorie and sugar content of a fruit salad.

Raw veggies:

Raw vegetables vary in their nutritional content, but here is some general information:

Carrots: Rich in vitamin A and potassium, they also contain vitamin C, folate, and fiber.

Cucumbers: Low in calories and high in water content, they are a good source of vitamin C and potassium.

Bell peppers: High in vitamins A, C, and B6, and potassium.

Tomatoes: Good source of vitamin C and lycopene, an antioxidant that may reduce the risk of certain types of cancer.

Broccoli: High in fiber, vitamins C, A, and K, and potassium.

Zucchini: Low in calories and rich in potassium and vitamin C.

Celery: Low in calories, high in water content, and a good source of vitamin C and potassium.

It is important to note that cooking and processing can alter the nutritional content of vegetables. Raw vegetables generally retain more of their vitamins and minerals than cooked ones.

Yogurt

The nutritional information for strawberry chia seed yogurt can vary depending on the brand and ingredients used, but here is a general estimate based on a serving size of 8 ounces (237 ml):

Calories: 140-150

Fat: 2-4 g

Saturated Fat: 1-2 g

Cholesterol: 5-10 mg

Sodium: 60-80 mg

Carbohydrates: 20-25 g

Fiber: 3-5 g

Sugar: 12-15 g

Protein: 8-10 g

Vitamin D: 2-5% of the daily recommended value

Calcium: 20-25% of the daily recommended value

Iron: 2-4% of the daily recommended value

Potassium: 4-5% of the daily recommended value

It is important to note that chia seeds are a good source of omega-3 fatty acids and antioxidants, which can benefit heart health and reduce inflammation in the body.

Nut

The nutritional information for Maple Cinnamon Roasted Almonds can vary depending on the brand and the specific recipe used. However, here is a general nutritional information for a serving size of 28 grams (1 oz) of roasted almonds:

Calories: 160

Fat: 14g

Saturated Fat: 1g

Trans Fat: 0g

Cholesterol: 0mg

Sodium: 0mg

Carbohydrates: 6g

Fiber: 3g

Sugar: 3g

Protein: 6g

Note: This information is just an estimate and should not be taken as professional medical advice. The actual nutritional content of Maple Cinnamon Roasted Almonds may vary based on the preparation method and the ingredients used.

Rice cracker

A typical rice cracker serving size of about 20-25 crackers contains:

Calories: 120-130

Fat: 2-3g

Saturated Fat: 0-1g

Trans Fat: 0g

Cholesterol: 0mg

Sodium: 200-300mg

Carbohydrates: 25-27g

Fiber: 0g

Sugar: 1-2g

Protein: 2-3g

Note: Nutritional information can vary based on the brand and flavor of the rice cracker.

CHAPTER NINE

Staying on Track

Staying on track after following a 1200 calorie diet can be challenging, but it is possible with some effort and dedication. The following are some recommendations to help you stay on track:

Keep a food diary: Writing down what you eat can help you track your progress and make it easier to stay within your calorie limit.

Plan your meals: Plan your meals in advance and stick to your plan as much as possible. This will help you avoid impulse eating and make sure you are getting all the nutrients you need.

Eat plenty of vegetables: Vegetables are low in calories but high in fiber and nutrients, making them a great choice for weight management. Try to include a variety of colorful veggies in your meals.

Drink water: Water is essential for hydration and can help fill you up, reducing the urge to snack.

Avoid sugary drinks: Sugary drinks are high in calories and can contribute to weight gain. Rely on water, unsweetened tea, or coffee instead.

Exercise regularly: Exercise can help boost your metabolism and reduce stress. On most days of the week, Try to work in with at least 30 minutes of light activity often these days of the week.

Get enough sleep: Lack of sleep can affect your hormones, making it harder to control your appetite and maintain a healthy weight. Sleep for 7-8 hours every night.

Aim to eat mindfully: Enjoy each bite of food by paying close attention to it. This will help you avoid overeating and stay within your calorie limit.

Remember, weight loss is a slow process and it's important to be patient and consistent. Stick to your plan and give yourself time to adjust to the changes.

Strategies for success

Here are some strategies for success in maintaining a healthy lifestyle:

Set realistic goals: Start by setting achievable goals, such as drinking more water or eating more fruits and vegetables. Once you achieve these goals, set new ones to continue your progress.

Create a support system: Surround yourself with people who support your goals and can help keep you accountable. This might be a friend, a member of your family, or a group online.

Find healthy alternatives: Instead of cutting out your favorite foods completely, find healthy alternatives that can still provide the same satisfaction. For example, try using Greek yogurt instead of sour cream or using avocado instead of mayonnaise.

Keep a food diary: Keeping a food diary can help you stay on track with your eating habits and track your progress.

Plan your meals: Plan your meals in advance to help you stay within your calorie limit and avoid impulsive eating.

Stay active: Regular exercise is essential for maintaining a healthy weight and improving your overall health. Try to incorporate physical activity into your daily routine, even if it's just a walk around the block.

Practice mindfulness: Pay attention to your food and savor each bite. This can assist you in choosing healthier foods and preventing overeating.

Get enough sleep: Lack of sleep can affect your hormones and make it harder to control your appetite and maintain a healthy weight. Make an effort to rest for 7-8 hours a night. Remember, success takes time and consistency. Don't be too hard on yourself and celebrate your small victories along the way.

Handling cravings

Handling cravings can be challenging, but there are strategies that can help:

Drink water: Drinking water can help fill you up and reduce the urge to snack. Try to drink a glass of water before reaching for food.

Distract yourself: Find something to do that takes your mind off food, like going for a walk, reading a book, or watching a movie.

Practice mindfulness: Pay attention to your hunger levels and be mindful of your cravings. Ask yourself what might be causing the craving and if there are healthier alternatives you can reach for instead.

Get enough sleep: Lack of sleep can affect your hormones and make it harder to control your appetite. Make an effort to rest for 7-8 hours a night.

Eat healthy, filling foods: Eating foods that are high in fiber and protein, such as vegetables, nuts, and whole grains, can help you feel full and reduce cravings.

Use affirmations: Tell yourself repeatedly that you are in control of your life and that you are choosing to make healthy decisions."

Have a healthy snack: If you're feeling a craving, try reaching for a healthy snack like fruit, veggies, or nuts. This can help you avoid reaching for less healthy options.
Remember, cravings are normal, and they will pass. Stay committed to your goals and remind yourself of the benefits of making healthy choices.

Incorporating physical activity into your routine

Incorporating physical activity into your routine is important for maintaining a healthy weight and overall health. Here are some tips for making it a part of your routine:

Make it fun: Choose an activity you enjoy, like dancing, swimming, or hiking, to make it more enjoyable.

Set a schedule: Schedule time for physical activity every day, like a morning walk or a workout after work.

Get a workout partner: Having a workout partner can make exercise more enjoyable and help keep you motivated.

Use technology: Take advantage of fitness apps and wearable technology to track your progress and stay motivated.

Mix it up: Try different types of physical activity to avoid boredom and prevent burnout. This could include yoga, weightlifting, or cycling.

Find short, quick activities: If you're short on time, find short, quick activities that can be done throughout the day. This could include taking the stairs instead of the elevator or doing a quick workout during your lunch break.

Make it a family affair: Involve your family in physical activity, like going for a walk or playing sports together.

Turn chores into exercise: Make your daily chores into physical activity, like sweeping the floor, washing the car, or mowing the lawn.

Remember, it's important to find physical activity that works for you and that you enjoy. simply start out slow and gradually up the duration and intensity of your exercises.

CONCLUSION

Summary of benefits

A calorie-controlled diet can offer many benefits for your health, including:

Weight loss: By reducing your calorie intake, you can lose weight and improve your body composition.

Improved metabolism: By consuming fewer calories, your body will work harder to metabolize food, which can help boost your metabolism.

Better heart health: A calorie-controlled diet can help reduce your risk of heart disease and improve your overall heart health.

Better blood sugar control: A calorie-controlled diet can help regulate your blood sugar levels, which can be especially beneficial for people with diabetes.

Improved mental health: Eating a balanced, calorie-controlled diet can improve your mood and reduce the risk of depression and anxiety.

Increased energy levels: By eating a balanced, calorie-controlled diet, you can improve your energy levels and reduce feelings of fatigue.

Better digestion: A calorie-controlled diet can improve digestion and reduce the risk of digestive problems like bloating, constipation, and diarrhea.

Better sleep: By eating a balanced, calorie-controlled diet, you can improve your sleep and reduce the risk of sleep disorders.

Remember, it's important to consult with a doctor or registered dietitian before starting a calorie-controlled diet to ensure it's safe and appropriate for you.

Encouragement for success

Success in a calorie-controlled diet requires patience, perseverance, and determination. Here are some ways to stay encouraged and motivated:

Set realistic goals: Set achievable goals for yourself, and make a plan for how you will reach them. Celebrate each success along the way.

Keep a food diary: Write down what you eat and how you feel, so you can track your progress and identify patterns.

Surround yourself with support: Find friends, family, or a support group who will encourage and motivate you.

Find healthy substitutes: Find healthier substitutes for the foods you crave, so you don't feel deprived.

Treat yourself: Reward yourself for reaching milestones, like losing a certain amount of weight or making it a certain number of days without breaking your diet.

Stay active: Exercise is a great way to stay motivated and boost your confidence.

Keep a positive attitude: Remember that setbacks are a normal part of the process, and focus on the positives.

Educate yourself: Learn about healthy eating and lifestyle habits to better understand the benefits of a calorie-controlled diet.

Seek help: If you find yourself struggling, reach out to a doctor, dietitian, or therapist for help.

Remember, success takes time, and everyone moves at their own pace. Maintain focus on your goals and don't give up!

Final thoughts and tips.

A calorie-controlled diet can be a great way to achieve a healthier weight and improve overall health. However, it's important to remember that success requires patience, dedication, and a commitment to making healthy choices. Here are some final tips for success:

Stay balanced: A calorie-controlled diet should be balanced, with a variety of nutrient-dense foods.

Hydrate: Drink plenty of water to stay hydrated and support your metabolism.

Avoid processed foods: Processed foods are often high in calories, salt, and unhealthy fats. Choose whole, unprocessed foods instead.

Get enough sleep: Aim for 7-8 hours of sleep each night to support your health and metabolism.

Manage stress: Stress can trigger overeating and poor food choices. Find healthy ways to manage stress, like meditation or exercise.

Don't skip meals: Skipping meals can disrupt your metabolism and lead to overeating later. Aim to eat 3 balanced meals and 2-3 snacks each day.

Be consistent: Consistency is key to success on a calorie-controlled diet. Make healthy choices every day, and stick to your routine.

Don't compare yourself to others: Everyone's journey is different, so focus on your own progress and celebrate your own successes.

Ask for help: If you find yourself struggling, reach out to a doctor, dietitian, or therapist for support.

Remember, success on a calorie-controlled diet takes time, but it's worth it for the benefits to your health and wellbeing. Stay focused, stay motivated, and keep making healthy choices!

Made in the USA
Las Vegas, NV
26 November 2023

81524447R00066